STEF PIXNER

*Sawdust
and White
Spirit*

To my mother and my brother

Published by VIRAGO PRESS Limited 1985
41 William IV Street, London WC2N 4DB

British Library Cataloguing in Publication Data

Pixner, Stef
  Sawdust and white spirit.
  I. Title
  821'.914   PS3566.I9/

  ISBN 0-86068-710-4

Printed in Great Britain by
Anchor-Brendon, Tiptree, Essex
Photoset by Rowland Phototypesetting Ltd
Bury St Edmunds, Suffolk

Some of the poems in this collection have appeared in *Licking the Bed Clean*, *Smile Smile Smile Smile*, *Bread and Roses*, *Apples and Snakes* and *Big Bang*.

Contents

she's a trier
a night flier
lion tamer
town crier
trouble shooter
bloody liar

intimacy

fog days

and arctic nights
asleep
on other planets

raging days

when a cup
or a footstep
forks my tongue

peacock days

in colours
dressed
to kill

*my love has white arms
and many faces*

*I deal a tricky pack of hearts
and aces*

we smile
and wave
but do not find
us

all our rubies
glitter to blind
us

Possibility

I'm standing here naked on this mountain washing myself
                                                    all over
my feet in wild oats and mint.
It's very hot and I'm washing myself with a hosepipe shower
                                            and thinking
about the impossibility of my life in London
about the impossibility of my life
anywhere except here where nothing seems impossible because
when I bend to wash my hair wild oats come up to meet me and
the blue afternoon mountain
                                    turns upside down.

I return

I return
from a land of rock and water
(when the rain falls there
you can see the sky)
to this brick city
to this screeching city
to this spread out swarming city
so elegant, so decrepit
my home

I return
from nights of soft sleep
and days of slow living
to find
a baby in my belly
bombing in Beirut
and a pile of unsorted mail

The men I live amongst
have vacated their eyes
the stairs are dusty
and newspapers creep
across the kitchen floor

I like being pregnant

I like my breasts
that have soared
from hill to mountain
and the father
who laughs when I tell him
and holds me in his arms

Under the sunbrown skin
a cluster of cells
swells
secretly
red as a raspberry
bedded in blood

Returning to this city
so choked, so spacious
(where even the clouds
look tailored in Kensington
and cancerous in Kings Cross)

I look up information
about 'termination'

The cement mixer

The cement mixer
sleeps in the hall.
Pretend it's the stereo
says the builder
and the skip is a junk
in a Chinese river
and the lorries
are the juggernaut ocean
roaring
or lions
hunting a dusty jungle,
the Dalston Junction
of the soul

high heeled sneakers

i dreamed Simone de Beauvoir and i
were climbing a mountain eating crepes
and wearing espadrilles. she carried
her alarm clock on her head
whereas i pulled behind me three train
carriages full of the things i thought
i might need for the journey.
we talked pleasantly of this and that. i
was trying to impress her with how
interesting i was coming from the post
war generation from a communist family
and being a woman but i had to stop
every now and again to change my
espadrilles for ballet shoes or army boots
or pick my nose or adjust a comma
on my hat or look at the view
or a word in the dictionary so that
she got to the top of the mountain before
me despite her years and
ate more crepes in the meanwhile
sitting on her alarm clock and waiting
for me and my train. when i got
there at last she said there are some
questions i've been meaning
to ask a woman of your
generation and so she began asking me
questions and i changed from my
army boots to a pair of high heeled
sneakers and back to espadrilles and then
back into ballet shoes. i've been meaning
to write you a long letter i said but just
then we saw a horde of mountain bears make
off with the luggage i'd so carefully

chosen and she still had a few books
to eat that morning so we exchanged
espadrilles and chinese postcards and
waved our red handkerchiefs
just as the lights went up.

Prawn Creel Café, Kyle of Lochalsh

Every time someone opens the blasted door
the sea wind goes wild
across the coke bottles
wild over the sweet cold cans of Lilt
over the damp map
and the sodden anorak

Outside the window
masts of the ferryboat come and go
against the ghost of Skye
and the parked cars, and rain
gusts and squalls, and gulls
wheeling white
and the sea unseen
in rain
glowering low

Every time someone opens the blasted door
it kisses me
the sea wild wind
and carries the thick sweet smell of frying
over the sea to Skye

Elegy for a shabby café

Rain weeps
on the big corner windows

Nikos, man of troubles
brings in the milk
the semolina cake
the Mother's Pride

His uncle, the leaseholder
watches
the last of the chessboard wars

Grey light
on the grey formica

'For some people, an idea
can become like a bright star'
says Peran shyly
across the table: 'it dominates the sky'

First cup of coffee
I remember I'm alive

Doreen shuffles in
'I'm sorry I'm sorry'
fear written on her yellow fingers
'I had a letter from Mecca this morning
Have you got a cigarette?'

'It's like being in love'
croons the chessplayer
from Harlesden:
'with this move, I thee wed'

'Love!' snorts Paul
(who once was a big man)
'God is love.' He turns to Nikos:
'The trouble with you Greeks
you never had a Pope'

'Go back to Warsaw'
says Mike the Bike, surly
sliding a priest
along the chequered board

'No, go to America!'
says Nikos:
'it is full up
of disease'

The quiet American smiles and reads the *Guardian*
the tramp in the corner reads the *Sun*

Mr Kyprianos
smokes
and strokes
his face

Tomorrow
he will sell the lease
to a pay and run
Perfect Pizza
fast food place

'Who knows what's in a dog's mind?'
enquires the thin-haired van driver
adjusting his jacket

'How does religion come about?' he adds
addressing the ceiling
proceeding to prove in three moves
the non-existence of God

the Father, the Son, the Holy
Ghost, or any other unnatural, supernatural
product of our longing
for love

Mrs Churchmouse, whose feet
don't touch the floor
examines her pension book
and says nothing at all

'All my thoughts turn into prayers'
says Sylvester
(who is on six hundred milligrams
but flushes five hundred down the loo):
'layers and layers of prayers

I'm going to see the Doctor
see if he will let me out'
'Where will you go?' asks Doreen
'Heaven.' He nods his reply

Doreen rummages for dark glasses
to filter her fear

I write in my notebook:
I was happy here

'Money isn't power' Paul pronounces
'Course it is' says Mike the Bike
'It's funny but it's true
what a lollipop can do' sings the man
from Harlesden

Nikos cleans the ashtrays

soon he will be
king of a chip shop
by the sea

*Joie de Lire**

we wander through Paris
and our hair turns grey

inside the bookshop there's chaos;
a frenzy of mediations.
sentences from all over the world
leap from the shelves
green as sand, yellow as city streets,
dancing and arguing,
shouting slogans and reciting poetry
assaulting my brain cells
creating havoc in those tender circuits
of nerve and blood.

oh my head, imprisoned, exploding . . .
we're lost in this place
entangled in ourselves

the books
the pages
the hyphens
the full stops
the semi-colons

some unknown writer
beyond the publisher
the printer
the distributor
the bookseller
with broken toenails and insomnia
some unknown author
writing beside a mountain
where the blood flows

in the shadow of green grain
in the shadow of a gun;
hundreds of thousands of unknown authors
chewing their cigars
picking their noses
excreting one word after the next

        my nerves
        stretched over bright mirrors
        jangle of cash registers
        jangle of skin and bone

our love turns in circles
we live in a web
our faces reflect
over and over

        in café mirrors
        shining teapots
        in steel and in china
        in brown and in green

beware of pickpockets
of thieves, invasions, revolutions
beware of changes in the colour of the sky
                the skin
                the breasts
                the heartbeat
beware of your raw fingers, our indecision
of your clear sad eyes
      and my angry ones.

A big left-wing bookshop in Paris, now closed.

dogs, seagulls, umbrellas

every day i talk too much
it's my job
i get paid for it

at lunch
i go to a café near a park
i drink coffee, eat omelettes,
listen to other people talk

today i walked back through the park
the bare green grass
                    spread out wide as a fish eye lens
the grey sky billowed

i saw dogs
        seagulls
        umbrellas

the seagulls cried out
                    and chased the dogs
the umbrellas burst out
                    like butterflies

a slice of lemon-coloured light
opened up
            behind the high arching black trees
the skyline grew ominously crystal small

and then the rain came down down down down down

on the opposite side of the white stagecoach
a man with a hostile bunch of green bananas
began to wail and scream like a sea anemone
deserted by the sea or an umbrella without rain.
he began throwing the bananas
at the women passengers who waved their ears
at him saucily and stifled their mirth.

scarecrow

the scarecrow
looks sad tonight all covered in rags
her solitude made of sticks
flapping in the dark field
and her eyes that won't shut
watching the cows at sleep.
with no shoes
and wind in her pockets,
she counts those stars
she can see
from her fixed angle
and listens to the black sticks rubbing
as she spits her curses at the moon.

that world through the window
is a barefaced lie

---

that world
through the window
is a barefaced lie.

there is ink on the yellow fields
and the moon
has been glued to the night
like an egg in a scrapbook.

bitter the battering moth
and the grasses that wind
shaken wave.

bitter the bird that flies
in ever smaller circles
as the poisoned world contracts.

there is a cold wind
inside me
and a bird
flies like a black rag
over the fields
behind my eyes.

there was a child there
red berries biting the sky

in the hard light
in a glass world
banging against the glass

what is your name, child?
can you speak?

red berries biting
a glass sky, the white light
and the flat sound of the child,
                                    banging

Halfway House

We lived all together
and all apart
in a room
with three high windows

silence lay
stiff
under the noise of quarrelling

between our iron beds
only a chair:
'Turn your faces to the wall'
she'd say
'and go to sleep now'

She lived alone
in the same room
worn down by days
of typewriter keys

At night
the radio voices
came from somewhere lost
and black

I thought they must be lonely
the radio people
in their bakelite box

That's when things
began to pile up

I stole butter
as well as eggs
and daffodils
from gardens

yellow saves
I thought: it loves you
like the sun

Anything yellow

I'd find
and steal
and eat

Looking for a walnut tree

Thunder without rain
in Vienna

the trams rumble and ring

'Outside my window,' he had written
'stands a walnut tree

its leaves are scented and long'

All her life
the little girl knew
her daddy left her

Thin and brown and muscled
long-travelled

a virgin
with torn jeans and broken shoes

she searches white flats in the suburbs
looking for a walnut tree

she hasn't written
he has no phone

he doesn't know
she's tracked him down

What is a man
who is a daddy?

what is a daddy
to find
when never known?

Whose fault?

Then, you were the freckled saint
who sighed and froze

and I the sinner, always.

Outside, the claws of winter grip
the tree of heaven

a blizzard blinds the window
whipping quiet and white.

Inside, the tea is cold before it's poured
newspapers heap in deep drifts

like those in the road.
Cats scatter the landscape

of paper hills.

My memory plays like your cats
in the chaos

I remember days when the soup sloped south
and north where the warped table dipped

when your worn, warm lap
was haven; kisses noon and night

rabbit turds and Arthur's knights together
on a bald baked lawn.

But then your red unruly hair
fierce halo,

burned with blame.

Later I burned you too
I belched fire

for years I raked
charred bones.

You said I tried to kill you
I said you left me dead

you wronged me:
admit it! admit it!

A fault is a deep crack
a single seam splits and slips

awry, and the two sides subside
forever separate

whose fault
is it?

Your light eyes startle
blue as before

tho' your long ago carrots
have turned to snow.

The stove slowly warms the room

I take my coat off
sit back in my chair

look at the books
you've bought since I was here

you talk to me
of Moscow's boozers

and of Albania's ancient kings

and you laugh now
under the bare bulb

wavering over the depths,
no blame

it's with others
that now I burn and burn.

The king

I

Fierce he was

how I hated him
and worshipped

his beanpole legs
his stringy blue veined arms

that shoved my nose, like a cat's
to the floor:

it's your mess
wipe it up!

No.

I screamed for the neighbours
or I bribed him:

give me your toby jug
give me two-and-six

II

Sad he is

sorrow the colour
of his dark beard

hidden anger
his worms and his bread

father now, he is
and husband

duty his road
and narrow his bed

III

O come let us adore him
O come let us adore him

brother and father to me
power and glory to me

I must dethrone you now

IV

king of my heart

Near death

Near death
she halts

bent, brown, ninety
smelling rank.

She's peeled
the family photos

from the walls
leaving pale patches

bare of dust
like the rubbed out patches

of her memory.

'Is it Saturday today?
day or night, is it?'

At last she's happy
the bitterness of unlived passions

rubbed out too.

Cunningly young
she smiles, bends

fiddles a red rose through my button hole.
'My darling girl!'

Its sharp stalk
tickles the skin

between my breasts.

Grandmother Hubbard

She's beautiful and wicked
battering at the door

stealing secrets
from her husband's drawer

poking her nose
in her daughter's petticoats

and her fingers
in her granddaughter's head:

'Your friends aren't good enough
your mother has no heart

and why aren't you wearing red red red?'

But Grandmother Hubbard
keeps a full cupboard

she calls out in the evenings
over to the trains and the trees
where I squat in the mud:

'Come home to my safe garden
where the sun shines
and the cherries ripen

my little plum
come home'

But that was years and years ago

and now she's dead dead dead

the pain that I find in dust and disorder

the pain that I find
in dust and disorder
she carries on her back
like bread.

I asked for a ladder
for a gilded stagecoach
I asked for the moon

I found old tins in the cupboard
old tins, old dust
and her soft, soft skin.

fox colours of rust and brown
a nest of yellowed papers
and a bed full of books.

she gave me bunches
of words on a keyring
and question marks
to open locked doors.

the pain that I find
in dust and disorder
she carries on her back
like bread.

choice: the cutting edge

I

there's a rock in my pocket
cuts a hole in my jacket

II

panic. the world's unsafe
my belly knows it.
better to sleep forever
without a charming
spellbreaker

III

alone
in the dry river
bed of my worst
fears she told me;
'pick up a stone'.

smooth and bald
safe as eggs
the rock of ages
nestled
perfect in my hands;
no finger hold
no crack
to let me in.

IV

I smashed it;
like a cup it cracked
on the stones.

the sharp pieces
cursed me,
their raw edges and
silver veins
glittered
angry as secrets

V

and I saw
blood
at the edge
of the flickering screen.

love poem

I love all the fat bits of you
and the hairy bits
and the smooth round silky masses of you
and the light inside you when you shine
and your serious obsessional mind
reaching out for the moon and totality
and your white legs in red slippers
and your clear eyes and your stories
and your dominance and your submission
and the feeling of your presence
and your warm arms
and you

mugshots: before and after

I

four sullen photographs
fall from the chute

my jaw says (four times)
'I hate you for going'

II

I see you wave
clear and small at the end
of the bridge between train and plane

there was scarlet paint
sharp sunlight
the ticket collector's cap

III

last week in the same booth
we kissed for the camera

now I hold our love
in a strip. four snaps

between two fingers
                    smile
                    smile
                    smile
                    smile

the second toothbrush, is it hers?
or do you have two now
you brought mine back?

why is it the toothbrush
that hurts
the worst?

The break-up

For years

I wore you
like an old slipper

Now my fists
break

on your wooden
face

and my guitar
plays grief

Santa Fe

The iron bell strikes four times

the light on the mud walls
quiet as your face
reminds me of you

In my dream you sat in a church
and cried
for your lost God

I never believed
in that faraway father
that imaginary friend

I believed in leaves
and lampposts
and the family of man

here I have lost all that

I am empty
like you
when we first met

The church bell strikes
behind me now

along the mountain road

absence

birdless days

the street wiped up like a frosty plate
windows rimed with cold white feathers

absence of leaves
absence of twilight

a cough echoes across puddles like iron

I wait for a letter like I wait for leaves

with hot house flowers
in my ungloved hands.

snake

along the cold street
a snake is marching
without boots
in silent slime
whistling a reptilian
melody in moving
scales.

it's night and only i
can hear its song and see it
slithering
with my shut eyes

no one is about
except this snake and me

and i'm sneezing.

camping alone

crossing stiles
thinking of no one
pitching a tent
striking it
thinking of no one
watching the river
slide
under the bridge
cooking
in a faraway field
changing a gas canister
thinking of no one

deep shade under the yew trees
dark ones
ancient ones
thinking of no one
deep shade
deep rest

morning;
in my bowl
green light.
sky burns
turns through
blue silence.
every real sound
falls
on open ears.
i go down now
to the sea
without doubts.

train and the river

riverrace swollen lace poisoned foam cold screaming
five o'clock whistle blowing your face like an old
blue eyed mountain craggy with straw beard running
along by the ice black flood river jumping
from sleeper to sleeper those huge chunks of grey
wood the iron rails quiet beside the surging
spring water and under the sleeping black train

a row
of peerless
icicles

think lucky

I

sunset falls
like blood
on the clockface

smell
of pepper and pine
and fresh rain

II

he says
think lucky

i say
the world is outside
your will

and mine

III

(tho' we may
act
on it)

IV

for ten dollars
he sells his blood
wears out his shoes
looking for the lucky break

V

i feel panic
in downtown cafés

he sees
the fear rise
says run
we'll outwit
it

grabs my hand

we leave fear
behind
on Telegraph Hill

VI

Christmas chronicle:

the newspapers
reek of death

Shah's troops
kill mourning
masses
in Iran

thirty-three dead
boys
found under
ranch house home, Chicago
(the smell
of excavation
is terrible)

Guyana:
900
cyanide suicides
terminate
such an excess
of hope

VII

he says
it's a lack of love
in the world

i say
perhaps

it boils down
to that

VIII

after a lot
of boiling

IX

sunset stains
the clock face

i think lucky
(just in case)

52

skin deep

tight as a button
loose as thread
bloody as words
which leak from my head

sticky and sucking still
how the lily tongues cry
sticky and spitting pretty
for beauty we live, for beauty we die

only skin deep, we know it within
but how many words can dance on a pin
and somebody tell us, please:
how deep is skin?

term begins again (ostrich blues)

I find myself
in bed again
with the sheets up over
my head again

papers collect
on my desk again
reports and memos and lists again

there are the
timetables in black ink
again

the silhouetted heads
in rows against the light
again

the lists again
of books I haven't read
again

nightmares again
of assignations missed
again

of students riding off
on bicycles playing bass guitars
again

and I oversleep
                again
                and again

I find myself
in bed
again

with the sheets up over
my head

again

A day in the life . . .

Today I cleared out the kitchen with Dougie so Hedley could sand the kitchen floor.

It was a Saturday today. Sun came through the window squares and lit up the dust.

Today I smoked cigarettes I didn't want to smoke.

I washed up meticulously; plates, bowls, cups, cutlery, pans. I wiped the draining board and emptied the crumbs from the drawers.

Today Dave and I fucked but I didn't want to kiss him because his mouth tastes funny in the morning.

Today I felt nauseous with grey anxiety as we drove to buy a reconditioned vacuum cleaner, Dougie and I. The sky turned grey, too, in the world outside the car.

Today my room was calm as a temple. The cat came in it for the first time for weeks.

Today I pulled my diaphragm out of my vagina. I found a small basin of dark blood.

Today Rachel's face flooded with love. 'I'm jealous,' she said with a mischievous and defiant certainty. I watched her face harden and soften by turns.

Today my fingers itched to play the guitar and I found myself singing a song.

Today I was delighted to find a jar of whole nutmegs; I had thought that we had no nutmegs.

Today my orgasm was frantic and elusive like the pot of gold at the rainbow's end.

Today I gave Lisa a massage, and I liked the feel of her back.

Today pains gripped either side of my neck like oak tree roots or eagle's claws.

Today I wrote a list of complaints. I'll act on them later.

Today with Dougie, I carried out the heavy oak table and the fridge, slippery with years of egg drippings and grease.

Today Dave licked my belly button and I had a funny sensation somewhere far down inside.

Today I lay in a deep green bath with my toes sticking out at the end, between the taps.

Afterwards, I put on a clean white shirt.

Today Gillian introduced me to a group, according to whose information bureaucratic omissions and half truths are converted into hard facts. She works for the group at home.

Today I spilled blood on the bathroom floor. I wiped it up without a trace.

Today Dave bought a Chinese flute although he's stony broke. I said to Rachel: 'I want to destroy his body!' and made a fist.

Today he looked at me with smiling eyes and I withdrew.

Today I crept near him fondly and he turned away.

He laid his head on my breasts and I put my arms round him. Then he went out and I took up my pen.

Today I saw flecks of yellow in his eyes.

Today I noticed my hands gesturing in the air, giving my words a dancing shape.

Today I loved my lover's thighs, and the innocence of his bum.

Today I smelled sawdust and white spirit and dreamed that I gave up art for the sake of flattery.

Friendship

I have hated my friend for two days now.
I have decided she is a witch.
She has gone down to the river in bare feet
and a pink silk dress
and
I am alone with the outraged cicadas
sitting in the shade
of the house we have borrowed
reading a detective novel set in Glasgow
in the snow and thinking about how rarely women
kill.
I could blaze the trail.
Or
I could go down to the river
in my T-shirt
and new denim shorts
with some pink geraniums
and some fresh
bread.

Attic room

Once it was a boat
with green sails

now when the moon circles
the walls intercept

it's too big, this room,
too beautiful, too new

it was a boat
you built it

with Bob of the heavy boots
and heavy sighs

you pulled the old roof down
and exposed the sky

black-faced, white-eyed
and angry from soot

you rigged up
a tarpaulin

tying ropes like sailors
as a storm charged in from the south

it was hot then
floorboards were missing

and walls
the tarpaulin made a green light

I lay down in the heat one Sunday
on a pile of plasterboard

and imagined
making love to you

I never believed it would be a real room
that I would live in it

that I would make love in it
with you

on the floor
by the fire
in cold winter

when the boat was grounded
and the sails were down.

The right train

We walked by the canal
and the sun was eerie:
'What kind of a tree is that?'
'The warehouses are derelict'
'I can still change my mind'

It took no time at all

The anaesthetist joked
when he couldn't find the vein
and when I woke
high as a kite
I fell in love with the Finnish nurse
whose moon face shone above me

I felt like a baby myself

learning the world
for the first time.
Even the strip lighting
was a miracle
and the paint cracking
across the ceiling

You sat by the bed with plums
talking about your childhood
and we played 'I spy'

After the abortion
I got my brain back
colours had interest again
I stopped eating tomatoes
and my breasts
relaxed

But sometimes
I dream
that I've missed the right train

To go back one stop
I must first go to Tadzikistan
and though no one's information
can be trusted
I go on asking strangers
how to get back

like I go on walking with you
by the seed-covered
weedy canal;
'What kind of a tree is that?'
'The warehouses are derelict'
'I can still change my mind'

by tower bridge

midsummer
midnight

our legs
dangle
over
the wall

a pleasure boat
blazes
then fades
back
into black

two boats
moored
midstream
circle
and creak

you're
a silent ship
no lights
no foghorn
not passing
in the night

we're moored
alongside
ropes creaking
in the dark